SUPERMAN THE COMING OF ATLAS

JAMES ROBINSON
Writer

RENATO GUEDES
Penciller

WILSON MAGALHÃES
Inker

HI-FI
Colorist

ROB LEIGH
JOHN J. HILL
Letterers

ALEX ROSS
Original series covers

AND

ATLAS THE GREAT

JACK KIRBY
Writer and penciller

D. BRUCE BERRY
Inker and letterer

SUPERMAN THE COMING OF ATLAS

Dan DiDio Senior VP-Executive Editor
Matt Idelson Editor-original series
Nachie Castro   Tom Palmer, Jr. Associate Editors-original series
Bob Harras Editor-collected edition
Robbin Brosterman Senior Art Director
Paul Levitz President & Publisher
Georg Brewer VP-Design & DC Direct Creative
Richard Bruning Senior VP-Creative Director
Patrick Caldon Executive VP-Finance & Operations
Chris Caramalis VP-Finance
John Cunningham VP-Marketing
Terri Cunningham VP-Managing Editor
Amy Genkins Senior VP-Business & Legal Affairs
Alison Gill VP-Manufacturing
David Hyde VP-Publicity
Hank Kanalz VP-General Manager, WildStorm
Jim Lee Editorial Director-WildStorm
Gregory Noveck Senior VP-Creative Affairs
Sue Pohja VP-Book Trade Sales
Steve Rotterdam Senior VP-Sales & Marketing
Cheryl Rubin Senior VP-Brand Management
Alysse Soll VP-Advertising & Custom Publishing
Jeff Trojan VP-Business Development, DC Direct
Bob Wayne VP-Sales

Cover by Alex Ross
Color reconstruction on ATLAS THE GREAT by Joe Ketterer

SUPERMAN: THE COMING OF ATLAS

DC Comics, 1700 Broadway, New York, NY 10019
A Warner Bros. Entertainment Company
Printed in USA. First Printing.

ISBN: 978-1-4012-2131-7
SC ISBN: 978-1-4012-2132-4

I was very young, it was long ago, and the memories that surround this particular recollection are dim. And yet this one stands out, very distinctly in fact. I was a boy who enjoyed comics — as I'm sure many if not all of the men now holding this volume did too growing up.

It was an interesting time to collect too, living in London, England as I then did. This was still a few years before the opening of the first specialty comic book store. This store called "Dark They Were and Golden Eyed" (name taken from the title of a Ray Bradbury short story) was, by the time I found out about it, located in St. Anne's Court off Wardour Street in an area of Soho, London known mainly for film, TV and commercial post production. (Now, based on dictionary definitions, you might imagine this thoroughfare to be either a: an area open to the sky and mostly or entirely surrounded by buildings, walls, etc. — or b: a short street. While nitpickers might argue in favor of one or other of these definitions, St. Anne's Court itself had the definite feel of an alley to it. "Dark They Were, Not Golden Eyed But Rather Smelling of Effluvia" might have been a better name for the shop.)

Nevertheless it was a wonderland to a boy who was just learning that there was a time lag between comics arriving in British newsagents and when they appeared on the racks in America (and more important, on the racks in Dark They Were who had them flown in so they arrived a mere few days after the Americans got them). And, I was to also learn, there were the elusive "import only" comics. These comics were published in America, but for some reason (as far as I was concerned at the time, the work of Satan himself) these books never made it across the Atlantic to England. Before I discovered this fact, I merely assumed some other kid beat me to that issue at the newsagents. These books were gold. Desired beyond a boy's wildest dreams.

So due to this, as well as the store's vast supply of Shadow (with Steranko covers), Avenger and Edgar Rice Burroughs paperbacks, this was the place I went to whenever I could. As a result I tended not to visit the newsagents as much, where their new arrivals already seemed stale and tired, having been for sale in Dark They Were for two months. But I was losing something in the process, something that as I look back I miss greatly and which directly pertains to the Kirby reprint that ends this volume and which I am truly honored my humble offering has been published with.

But before I get into specifics, let me digress yet again (it will all come together by the end — I hope). Years later, I am going to buy my comics from Forbidden Planet in London (the comic book store usurper who took Dark They Were's crown when it closed down). By this time, comic-related news was such that you pretty much knew everything about a comic before it came out. Now today with catalogue solicitations you know every cover too, which was not always the case then, but definitely was in the case of any highly anticipated book. You knew the cover to look for long before the actual comic hit the stands. As an example, back then you might not have known what the latest issue of *The Flash* looked like, but you knew what every cover for *Watchmen* was going to be. Another example — you might not know what to expect cover-wise for *All-Star Squadron*, but there were no surprises when it came to the covers of *The Dark Knight Returns*.

Except that isn't true.

For some reason — in England at least — the cover image for the fourth part of *The Dark Knight Returns* hadn't been shown all over. In fact I don't recall ever seeing it — until I walked up to the aforementioned Forbidden Planet store and saw the cover to Issue #4 in the window. And I felt a thrill not experienced since those earlier times of newsagents and never knowing what to expect until you saw it.

Don't get me wrong, I love sitting on the toilet, reading my copy of the *Diamond Catalogue* as much as the next guy. But seeing the covers there — page after page of them — is no substitute for the excitement of stumbling across a new cover image on the actual comic, on the bottom shelf of a store selling newspapers, candy, women's magazines, *TV Guides* and tobacco. It's a time gone by, I guess. Oh well.

Anyway, let's deal with the specifics. This is several years before I encountered Dark They Were and Golden Eyed, and so discovering new comics was very much a treasure hunt. I was living in Kilburn, an area in the North West of London, but I remember the newsagent in question was in Willesden, a neighboring area. It was Saturday. I went into the place, as I recall for a chocolate bar, not comic books at all, which for me was extraordinary. And that's when I set eyes upon the first issue of *First Issue Special*. This was DC's new version of *Showcase* — a new comic book idea every month (or a reworking of an old idea). Apart from the advantage of a new Number One, I'm not sure why DC didn't just keep *Showcase* going, but there you go. Anyway, the first new idea was by the King of Comics, Jack Kirby himself. ATLAS, the featured villain in this, my first arc of Superman. The cover was big, bold Kirby. Everything you'd expect from a character that had echoes of Thor, Hercules and the "gods." The story itself, while not on par with his Fourth World, had a lot of the same elements of epic bizarre grandeur that were in his earlier work at DC.

I selected him as one of Superman's villains because I felt Superman's rogues gallery lacked a character that was the flip side of him in terms of his physicality. Yes, there's Doomsday, but he's hardly a guy you could discuss the finer points of Kierkegaard with while you were arm-wrestling him. Not that Atlas will ever be asked to join anyone's Algonquin Round Table, but he could at least discuss the finer points of chariots. I promise to make Atlas into a character you'll love — or at the very least love to hate. I have said on prior occasions that he'll be Superman's "Namor" — although where Namor's more extreme actions still remain just on the side of good, Atlas's will always fall just on the side of bad. But he will have heart and spirit and in that way be true to the Kirby one-shot that accompanies my arc.

Can I also take this moment to thank Renato for his work? These were early days for us — the start of our association — and I was especially impressed at that time by the way he hardened Atlas's face/form in our reality while giving him the clean, handsome lines of Kirby in the flash-back pages where he emulated the King's drawing style.

Oh, and where above I cited the reasons for selecting Atlas as one of Superman's foes, I'm lying. It was the memory of stumbling across that Kirby cover in a newsagent in Willesden.

James Robinson, Hollywood, December 2008

AND HE DOES THING MAKES *KRYPTO* HAPPY.

GOOD BOY.

HAPPY!

THIS IS *WEIRD*.

NO, THIS IS *FUN.*

NO. THIS IS *WEIRD.*

PLAYING FRISBEE--

--WITH MASKS AND COSTUMES AND POWERS--

YEAH, BUT--

NO, WAIT, I'M *NOT* DONE.

--IN SPACE WITH A SUPER-POWERED *CANINE*--

--IS *WEIRD.*

HAL, I THOUGHT *BETTER* OF YOU.

WHAT *ALL* HAVE YOU SEEN? HOW *MANY* WORLDS?

HOW *MUCH?* MAN, HOW MANY ALIEN *GIRLS* ALONE--ALL EXOTIC LOOKS AND SKINS AND SUCH--HAVE YOU *DATED?*

NOT AS *MANY* AS PEOPLE THINK.

WHAT ABOUT *JADE,* ALAN'S DAUGHTER? EXOTIC.

SURE. *VERY.* BUT THAT WAS KYLE.

LUCKY KYLE.

THEN. SURE. LUCKY. HIS--HER-- *THEIR* LUCK RAN OUT.

IT *TENDS* TO--WITH US.

CATCH.

ME. I SOUND *STUPID. SMUG.* TALKING ALL ROSES AND HEARTS AND FLOWERS AND *ROSES--BUT--*

I THINK I *BROKE* THE CURSE.

I HAVE LOIS.

LOIS.

OH YEAH, AND I HAVE THE BESTEST, GREATEST, MOST *WONDERFUL* DOG IN THE *COSMOS.*

FATE *THROWS* CURVEBALLS.

YEAH, FOR ME-- LIKE YOU--A *LOT* OF CURVEBALLS.

A LOT.

BUT I HAVE *LOIS* IN MY LIFE--AND A *DOG*.

A *GOOD* DOG.

AND THAT *GIVES* ME A LIFE. COMPLETE.

BOTTOM LINE, WHAT COULD GO *WRONG?*

HAL JORDAN--THE MAN BEHIND THE MASK AND GREEN POWER AND THE LAW IN *SPACE SECTOR 2814*--

--REMEMBERS A LIFE.

TEST PILOT. THE LOVE OF CAROL FERRIS.

VILLAINS *EASILY* BEATEN AND *MERRY* LAUGHTER AS AN EPILOGUE.

BEFORE STAR SAPPHIRE.

BEFORE PARALLAX.

BEFORE HIS LIFE *WENT* THE WAY OF PILOTS WHO *DIDN'T* PULL UP OR BANK OR LOOP OR LAND WITH THE *RIGHT STUFF.*

HAL JORDAN OF SPACE SECTOR 2814 LOOKS AT HIS FRIEND AND THINKS--

HE THINKS--

"HOW CAN THE *GREATEST MAN* IN THE GALAXY BE *SO NAIVE?*

"ALTHOUGH--

"--PERHAPS THAT'S WHAT MAKES HIM THE *GREATEST MAN.*

"HE HAS *FAITH.* HE BELIEVES IN SOMETHING *BETTER.*

"AND HIS DOG IS--

"--WONDERFUL."

HAPPY.

"MAYBE, HE'S RIGHT.

"WHAT CAN GO WRONG?"

THURSDAY IS MY FAVORITE DAY.

SO SAYS TRAVIS DuBARRY.

NO REASON WHY. IT JUST *IS.*

SOME OF THESE GUYS-- MY MEN--ARE *HARDCORE!*

GOTHAM COPS--EX-- KEYSTONE. OPAL. THEY'VE FOUGHT THE *WORST.*

AND *NOW* THEY'VE DONNED S.P. ARMOR TO FIGHT THE WORST, *WORST--*

--AS *ONLY* METROPOLIS CAN PROVIDE. THESE MEN EXPECT ME TO *LEAD* THEM. *ME.*

I *RUN* DOWN THE LIST IN MY HEAD--THEIR *NAMES*--I HAVE TO KNOW THEM, BACK AND FORTH KNOW THEM--

--*WHO* THEY ARE--*HOW* THEY ARE--

YEAH.

MCCAFFERTY, ADAM. BIG. REPORT SAYS HE BEAT A *ROCKET RED* ONE ON ONE. *ONCE* UPON A--*GOD* KNOWS WHEN. YEAH, BIG AND *NO* SMILES.

NOT FOR ME.

DASH, CAROL. TOUGH. HARDER THAN A LOT OF THE GUYS. HARDER *LOOKING*, TOO.

BUT I *THINK* SHE THINKS I'M COOL. I THINK.

SO I'M KICKED THIS JOB, OVER THE HEADS OF THE MCCAFFERTYS AND DASHES AND WHO ALL ELSE, WITHOUT *ANYONE* THINKING TO ASK WHETHER I'M *UP* TO THE TASK.

TRAVIS?

TROUBLE *IS* I SEE *WHAT* I AM--LUCKY, RIGHT PLACE, *RIGHT* TIME, WITH A SENATOR UNCLE AND A BLOODLINE BACK TO THE *MAYFLOWER*--

HOW'S IT GOING?

FINE, CONTROL. JIM DANDY.

THAT'S NOT WHAT OUR *CAMS* REPORT.

AH, THE *ALL-SEEING* CAMS.

AND THERE'S NO SIGN OF *SUPERMAN?*

MET.SP. 01

AH, THE ALL-SEEING, HEARING, *SMELLING* SUPERMAN.

NO STREAK OF RED AND BLUE YET, CONTROL. NO "HERE I COME TO SAVE THE DAY!".

BUT *BASED* ON YOUR ASSESSMENT, WE CAN BUT *PRESUME,* ASSUME, CONCLUDE YOU'RE *FURTHER ALONG* IN COUNTERING THIS MENACE THAN WE *MIGHT,* UPON INITIAL EVIDENCE *PERCEIVE?*

LIKE I SAID--

YES, JIM DANDY.

I *HAVE* TO DO SOMETHING--

TRAVIS *LICKS* HIS UPPER LIP AS HE THINKS THIS, TASTES THE *SWEAT.*

--SOMETHING *AMAZING--* SOMETHI--

SUPERMAN!

THE CREATURE'S *FLAILING* AS IT DIES--*CRAZY* AS IT DIES--*WOW*--

WHOA.

IT HIT THE *PLANET!*

THE *PLANET!*

NOT YOUR *FINEST* HOUR, SUPES.

CONTROL!
WE HAVE A
MAJOR--

19

GUILTY SECRET. I HATE SUPERMAN. NOT ALL THE TIME, NOT EVERY TIME, BUT--

--ALWAYS HERE, ALWAYS THERE, ALWAYS--

WE'RE SUPPOSED TO CLEAN UP AFTER HIM. PART OF THE JOB. CLEAN UP THE MESS.

SCIENCE POLICE. READY TO FIGHT. READY TO DIE. FOR THE JOB AND THE BADGE AND RIGHT OVER WRONG. WE'RE SPECIAL.

EXCEPT WHEN SUPERMAN MAKES US LOOK LIKE JANITORS.

YEAH, I HATE HIM, BUT--

--THAT WAS COOL.

SUPERMAN....!

WHERE **IS** HE? **WHERE** IS YOUR **TITAN**?!

I WILL SHOW HIM **SORROW**!

I WILL SHOW HIM **PAIN**!

I WILL SHOW HIM--

--ATLAS!

I AM THE **CHAMPION** THIS CITY, THIS LAND, THIS ORB **NEEDS**.

ME.

SO? WHERE **IS** HE?

I HAVE **NO** IDEA WHAT TO **SAY**.

GRIMALDI, ON THE **OTHER** HAND--

FREAK!!

22

GRIMALDI, JAKE. RASH. YOUNG. LATE OF THE *HUMAN DEFENSE CORPS.* SPENT TIME IN HELL IF *RUMORS* ARE TO BE BELIEVED. BRAVE. LOYAL.

BUT I RECALL HIS DOSSIER SAYING TACT *WASN'T* HIS BEST TRAIT.

HA! THIS IS BUT THE FROLIC OF *CHILDREN.*

WHY, I'VE FOUGHT AGING *CENTAURS* WHO HURT ME *MORE.*

OH YEAH?

MADISON, CLARE. CORPORAL. *COOL* UNDER FIRE.

SEXY TOO, TRUTH BE TOLD.

NOT THAT IT'S A *FACTOR* AT THIS MOMENT.

CAROL'S DOWN. I THINK HER ARM'S BROKE. THANK GOD IT'S *NOT* WORSE.

MCCAFFERTY, HARD MCCAFFERTY, GETS IT *HARDER*--

YUCK.

REPAIRS ON THE BIG GUY MIGHT NEED *ALLOY* TO BONE COME THE LIGHT OF *TOMORROW*.

AND NOW IT'S *MY* TURN.

THIS IS NONSENSE.

AND IT NEED NOT BE IN THE FIRST PLACE.

DON'T YOU SEE?

I WANT SUPERMAN!

SUPERMAN!

I HAVE TO GO, HAL.

TROUBLE?

SOMETHING.

LOOK AFTER KRYPTO.

I THOUGHT HE DIDN'T LIKE ANYONE BUT YOU.

HE'S CHANGED. HE'S A GOOD BOY NOW.

HAPPY.

FORCE-FIELD ENGAGED.

OH *GOOD*. THAT WORKED FOR, LIKE, A *SECOND*.

PLASMA.

CANNON.

LASER.

AND YOU CAN STICK A *FORK* IN THIS SAUSAGE.

THAT'S *ALL* I GOT.

27

LISTEN!

NOW.

PEOPLE OF METROPOLIS.

LISTEN.

I'VE COME A *LONG* WAY--

--FROM *LONG* AGO.

YES. I HAVE VENTURED.

THE DAILY PLANET BUILDING *LACKS* THE THING THAT MAKES IT SO UPON THE METROPOLIS SKYLINE.

A *SMALL* THING-- A SMALL CHANGE, AMONG MANY--

--THIS DAY.

HOW QUICKLY CAN WE GET THERE?

QUICKER ON *TWO* WHEELS THAN FOUR.

WE *LOST* THE DAILY PLANET, LOIS.

WE'VE LOST IT *BEFORE,* JIMMY, WE'LL GET IT BACK.

WHEN DID YOU GET THIS BIKE?

NOT MORE THAN A MONTH AGO. BUT I'VE KNOWN HOW TO RIDE FOR YEARS. I'D FORGOTTEN HOW *MUCH* I LOVE--

WHOA.

TIME TO *WALK,* LOIS.

I CAN SEE.

STILL, IT MEANS WE'RE *CLOSE* TO THE *ACTION.*

YEAH. CLOSE TO THE ACTION.

IT'S *FUNNY*. NOT LAUGH OUT LOUD FUNNY-- FUNNY LIKE--

--*SUPERMAN*. HIS MORNING. MINE WAS COFFEE, A SLICE OF PIE AND A *LITTLE* MORE COFFEE.

HE--

LOOK AT THE DUST THAT'S BEEN KICKED UP FROM *WHATEVER'S* GOING ON.

LOOK--

ANYWAY, I *WONDER*, SOMETIMES--

I MEAN-- SUPERMAN-- *HIS* MORNING.

WHERE'S *HIS* PIE AND COFFEE?

34

HE FLIES THROUGH A *MIST* OF VISIONS--

--WONDERFUL, *TERRIBLE*, THE WORLD GROWING, *CHANGING*, AGING THROUGH HIS EYES.

TOO MUCH, HIS MIND SAYS, *TOO MUCH*.

AND ATLAS SLEEPS.

HELLO, MY FRIEND. IT'S *TIME* TO WAKE UP AND *SMELL* THE COFFEE.

46

BEFORE I GO, TELL ME AGAIN HOW YOU BROUGHT ME HERE.

MY RESOURCES-- MONEY MOSTLY--ALLOW ME TO ACQUIRE SCIENCE. NOTHING SO FAR ENOUGH TO DEFEAT SUPERMAN MYSELF, BUT ENOUGH THAT MY ARSENAL IS FULL OF SPECIAL THINGS.

ONE TOY I COULDN'T BUY OUTRIGHT. BUT BRIBES AND AN INNOCENT LIFE OR TWO GOT ME IT ANYWAY, AND WITH IT I WAS ABLE TO FISH IN THE POOL OF TIME FOR A POWER SOURCE GREAT ENOUGH TO DEFEAT SUPERMAN.

IT FOUND YOU.

SO YOU STOLE ME TOO.

YES, I SUPPOSE--

NO. I HAVE A FEELING-- SOMEHOW--

--"YOU WERE GIVEN TO ME."

ATLAS, MY HERO.

--AND HIS *ROTTING* SKULL STILL ADORNS A *VANE* UPON THE ROOF OF ATLAS' SUMMER HOUSE BY THE WATER.

ATLAS TOOK HYSSA'S CITY AND *DEFENDS* IT WHEN HE MUST--

--BUT THE GOOD HAS *LEFT* HIM.

PEOPLE *FEAR* HIM AS *MUCH* AS THEY LOVE HIM.

THE THREE WHO ARE ONE. BRILLIANT AND *COMELY,* ONE OF THEM. ANOTHER *REMINDED* ME OF MY MOTHER. THE OTHER *FORETOLD* MY TWILIGHT.

WHO I THEN *BRIBED--*EASILY SO--FOR GOLD-HUNGRY MAGES EVER ARE, *NO MATTER* HOW BRILLIANT OR COMELY.

MY BRIBE? MY WISH?

I WOULD *NEVER* WANT MY LORD ATLAS DEAD, NO, I MERELY WISHED HIM *GONE.*

IN *SOME* WAY--

--THE MEANS THAT HE MIGHT *LEAVE* THIS WORLD *FOREVER.*

AND SO THE THREE WHO ARE ONE *CURSED* THE MOUNTAIN CRYSTAL SO THAT--

--AS IT *ENTERED* ATLAS' BODY--TO MAKE IT IN SOME WAY--

LIKE I SAID...YOU'RE TOUGH.

HE'S RUNNING.

NO WAY! NOT SUPES! HE'S--

DID YOU SEE THAT, LOIS?

SUPERMAN? DON'T WORRY. HE'LL COME BACK.

NO, I MEANT--UM-- I'LL TELL YOU LATER.

YEAH, SURE SUPES'LL COME BACK...

"...HE *ALWAYS* DOES."

THERE YOU ARE...

COME ON, THEN...

...LET'S HAVE YOU.

OH I'M *COMING*, BIG GUY.

ONE *LUCKY* PUNCH DOESN'T MARK THE *END* OF THIS.

...LET'S HAVE YOU.

ROUND *ONE* IS YOURS, MAYBE.

MAYBE.

BARRINGTON.

YES, MS. LANG?

DO YOU *SEE* WHAT'S HAPPENING ON THE NEWS?-- DOWN IN THE *STREET*?

IT APPEARS TO *ME* THAT SUPERMAN IS GETTING HIS ALIEN REAR RIGHTEOUSLY *HANDED* TO HIM ON A PLATE.

I *DON'T* LIKE THAT KIND OF TALK. UNDERSTOOD?

I GUESS. ALTHOUGH I *CONFESS* I'M NOT USED TO THAT BEING ONE OF THE *TERMS* OF MY EMPLOYMENT.

IT'S *CERTAINLY* NOT HOW WE DID THINGS WHEN MR. *LUTHOR* WAS HERE.

WELL *I'M* HERE NOW. IN FACT--

HOLD ON.

**** **** ** *****
********* ** * ******

HER FINGERS ON THE KEYBOARD, *FAST,* DONE IN MOMENTS.

THERE. *FINISHED.* NOW.

WE *HAVE* TO HELP SUPERMAN. IT'S OUR CIVIC DUTY.

I'M *SORRY* MS. LANG, I THOUGHT OUR *DUTY* WAS TO LEXCORP.

I'M GOING TO GET *TEAM LUTHOR* AIRBORNE.

FOR *WHAT,* MS. LANG? FOR *WHY?*

WHY? FILL IN FOR FALLEN SCIENCE POLICE, WHY. HELP SUPERMAN IN *ANY* WAY THEY'RE ABLE TO, WHY.

* **** *** *

SHE TAPS COMMANDS ON THE KEYS *AGAIN.* FAST AGAIN.

ONE OF THE ACTIONS VERY MUCH NOT AMONG YOUR CATALOGUE OF DUTIES WAS THE *ABETTING* OF ONE PARTICULAR ALIEN, *SUPERMAN* BY NAME.

BY *ATTEMPTING* TO ACTIVATE TEAM LUTHOR PERSONNEL TO AID THE KRYPTONIAN, YOU VIOLATED *PROTOCOL 13* IN YOUR EMPLOYMENT CHARTER.

EXCUSE ME, LEX, BUT *WHERE* IS THAT IN MY CONTRACT?

AH, LANA. I'M *DISAPPOINTED.* YOU'RE JUST LIKE *ALL* THE OTHERS AFTER ALL.

YOU *DIDN'T* READ THE FINE PRINT. VERY, *VERY* FINE PRINT.

THE *LAYMAN'S* VERSION OF IT BEING, HOWEVER -- THAT IF *ANY* LEXCORP EMPLOYEE, WHETHER WILLINGLY, UNWILLINGLY, KNOWINGLY OR NOT, ATTEMPTS TO HELP SUPERMAN, HERE IN METROPOLIS OR INDEED *ANYWHERE* IN THE WORLD, THEY WILL BE SERVED WITH *INSTANT* DISMISSAL. NO EXCEPTION FOR CIRCUMSTANCE OR RANK.

SO *BASICALLY* AT THIS MOMENT IN TIME--

--IT *SUCKS* TO BE YOU.

ALTHOUGH YOU *ARE* LUCKIER THAN IF THE *REAL* LEX LUTHOR WERE HERE.

I'M SURE HE--I--WOULD HAVE MY HANDS AROUND YOUR *THROAT* BY NOW.

SO *ALL* I CAN DO IS THANK YOU FOR YOUR *GENEROUS* SERVICE TO LEXCORP.

GOOD LUCK WITH YOUR FUTURE ENDEAVORS, *ALTHOUGH* YOU SHOULD KNOW THAT LEXCORP WILL DO *EVERYTHING* IT CAN TO IMPEDE THEM.

GOOD DAY.

WELL MS. LANG. IT LOOKS LIKE LEXCORP WILL *CONTINUE* TO DO BUSINESS THE WAY I'M USED TO, AFTER ALL.

THE *MORE* THINGS CHANGE, THEY MORE THEY STAY THE *SAME*, HUH BARRINGTON.

I'M *ASSUMING* FROM YOUR SMUG LOOK YOU'LL BE HAVING SECURITY ESCORT ME OUT OF HERE IN--WHAT'S THE USUAL?--FIFTEEN MINUTES?

NO, MS. LANG, I'M GIVING YOU *FIVE*. IN FACT THE ORDERS HAVE ALREADY BEEN SENT-- FURTHER TO IT THAT ANY *NON*-LEXCORP PERSON- NEL BE SHOT ON SIGHT *AFTER* THAT POINT.

FIVE MINUTES. I'LL GO THEN.

I WOULD IF I WERE YOU.

OH AND BY THE WAY, BARRINGTON, THE THING I DID *FIRST*... REMEMBER...ON THE COMPUTER, BEFORE I GOT MYSELF FIRED?

THAT WAS MY TELLING PERSONNEL TO FIRE YOU, TOO. YOUR "ALIEN" CRACK *REALLY* GOT TO ME.

FIVE MINUTES THEN SHOOT ON SIGHT, HUH?

HAVE *FUN* SPRINTING FOR THE DOOR.

YOU ARE NOT--

SIR, YES--I AM WATCHING IT-- AND WE'RE WINNING.

DID YOU SEE THAT?

WHAT?

I-- I--DON'T KNOW.

WHILE ELSEWHERE IN THE FINE CITY OF METROPOLIS--

SECOND BLUE AND RED, SIR.

INCOMING.

THE *GIRL*? OF COURSE.

SHALL I OPEN ROOM *FOUR*, SIR?

NO, I THINK ROOM THREE WILL *SUFFICE*, COLONEL.

KLK

HEY, I KNOW HIM.-- I THINK--I--

HIM?...

ERR. UM. AGAIN, LOIS--

...WHO HIM?

HOTEL 7734

ARE YOU LOCKED IN, COLONEL?

LOCKED IN, LOADED AND READY TO GO, SIR.

THEN LET THE LITTLE HUSSY *HAVE* IT.

NO.

NOT HER. NEVER--

KARA. YOU'RE HURT.

YES. AND I'M TAKING A *WILD* GUESS HERE, KAL, BUT *SO* ARE YOU.

NO TIME FOR JOKES, KARA.

NO--

FLY. *GO.* THERE'S *MORE* TO THIS.

ATLAS *ISN'T* ALL HE SEEMS.

THAT *RAY* FROM THE SKY THAT HIT YOU.

NO, KAL, I'M STAYING. TOGETHER WE--

NO TIME.

GO. PLEASE. *DO* WHAT I SAY.

IF I *DON'T*--

IF--

FIND THE TRUTH. FIND THE *ANSWERS*...

SUPERMAN WAS *HARDLY* THE FOE I WAS LED TO *EXPECT.*

AND *METROPOLIS.* A *SORRY* PLACE IF HE WAS ALL THIS CITY HAD.

217

OH, *THIS?*

AND *THAT?*

EXCUSE ME WHILE I HICCUP.

I HAVE TO SAY I'M *DISAPPOINTED.*

I WAS EXPECTING MORE *VALOR.*

I HOPED I'D MEET A *TRUE* HERO--

GRRR

Cover art to SUPERMAN #680

--CREATURE!

HURT--

--HIM!

HERE!

A **QUICK** DEATH!

BY ALL THE GODS.

A **QUICK** DEATH, INDEED. NEVER LET IT BE SAID ATLAS WASN'T MERCIFUL TO THE WORTHY.

STILL. WHAT A STUPID ANIMA--

HURT HIM!

--BUT *JEALOUS* WOULD BE A BETTER WORD, *TRUTH* BE TOLD.

HE'S *UNSTABLE,* CLARK. HE'S WILD.

HE'S MY DOG, LOIS. HE'S A *GOOD* BOY.

NO HE *ISN'T!* HE'S *FAR* FROM GOOD.

HE *DOESN'T* BELONG WITH US!

BY THE GODS, I'LL KILL Y--

BITE--

LOIS LOOKS AT A DOG--*NO*, A CREATURE IN HER EYES--

--SOMETHING THAT *SCARED* HER AND WHICH THE LOVE OF HER HUSBAND FOR IT MADE HER--SHE'D LIKE TO SAY UNEASY--

HELL, CLARK, HE *DOESN'T* BELONG ON *EARTH!*

LOIS WATCHES KRYPTO FIGHT A VILLAIN OF WHOSE POWERS SHE *HASN'T* SEEN THE LIKE--

--SINCE *DOOMSDAY.*

FOR THE *LOVE* OF HIS MAN.

FOR THE LOVE OF *HER* MAN.

HOW COULD I HAVE BEEN SUCH A *FOOL?*

HMM. *NOT* THE ENDING I EXPECTED, *NOR* DID I WANT IT SO.

BUT STILL--

GRRRRAA!

ER, SIR.

I SEE, GIVE HIM A DOSE FROM *ROOM 3.*

WHERE'S ZATANNA?

MY COUSIN--SHE'S OFF BEING HER *OTHER* SELF--ALL "SAVE THE WORLD, JUSTICE LEAGUE, SHADOWPACT, BLAH, *BLAH*"--DESTROY ONE DEVIL OR ANOTHER. CREEPY AND SCARY AND I *DON'T* KNOW WHY SHE DOES IT WHEN THERE'RE *EASY* GIGS LIKE THIS.

SO SHE'S NOT HERE?

IN A WORD, NO. *ZACHARY ZATARA* AT YOUR SERVICE. I'M HER STAND-IN.

ALTHOUGH AFTER TONIGHT, I *WON'T* BE.

DO I WANT TO KNOW WHY?

METROPOLIS, CITY OF TOMORROW, CITY OF *SCIENCE*. MAGIC--

--THAT LITTLE IMP WITH HIS DERBY HAT AND SILVER BANSHEE AND THEY'RE *NOT* HERE ALL THE TIME.

THAT MAKES ME A *BIG* FISH IN A VERY SMALL POND, WHICH I AM MORE THAN HAPPY TO BE. IN OTHER WORDS, MAN OF STEEL, GET USED TO METROPOLIS' MAN OF *MAGIC*.

MAN?

GIVE ME A FEW YEARS.

ALL RIGHT, "LITTLE MAN," *YOU'RE UP!* I NEED AN ARCANE SHIELD TO *PROTECT* ME FROM THE POWER OF A FOE WHOSE *STRENGTHS* ARE DERIVED FROM MAGIC TOO.

WHEN'S THE FIGHT?

OH, IT'S *ALREADY* STARTED.

THING IS, I'M *NOT* QUITE MY COUSIN IN TERMS OF HOCUS POCUS.

NOT QUITE, *HOW?*

INANIMATE STUFF, I'M BIG TIME.

LIVING THINGS, *NOT* SO GOOD.

GREAT. WHAT AN *ASSET* TO THE CITY YOU'LL BE. SO, WHAT? YOU'VE GOT *NOTHING* FOR ME?

LET ME THINK.

WHAT ABOUT THE SUN? I NEED THE *POWER* OF THE SUN.

SUN I CAN DO. I *THINK*. NO. YES. YEAH, I HAVE A SPELL FOR THE SUN. *BUT--*

BUT?

IT'S *STILL* INVOLVING YOU, BEING AN ANIMATE BEING, SO WHEN YOU FIGHT THIS THING, *MAN*, WHOEVER, *WHATEVER*, THE SPELL WON'T LAST FOR MORE THAN A *MINUTE*.

FROM THE *MOMENT* THE FIGHTING BEGINS?

THAT'S WHAT I SAID, ISN'T IT?

FRANKLY, I'M *NOT* SURE WHAT YOU SAID.

ANYWAY, *TIME* IS TIGHT. COME ON, LITTLE MAN OF MAGIC, LET'S *SEE* WHAT YOU CAN DO.

ZATANNA

ATLAS!

CAN YOU *HEAR* ME, METROPOLIS?

CAN YOU HEAR ME?!

YOU WANT TO *CHEER* A HERO?! *THIS* IS A *HERO!*

HE'S MY DOG. AND YOU KNOW *WHAT*--

--NOW HE'S *YOUR* DOG TOO.

BONUS FEATURE: FROM 1975, THE STORY

THAT SERVED AS THE INSPIRATION FOR

THE COMING OF ATLAS

THERE WERE GIANTS IN THOSE DAYS! ~AND THE MIGHTIEST OF THEM ALL WAS~

ATLAS THE GREAT!

CHAPTER ONE

A DC QUALITY MAGAZINE

EDITED, WRITTEN AND DRAWN BY~ JACK KIRBY
AND
INKS AND LETTERING BY~~~ D. BRUCE BERRY

1

THE SIGHTS IN THE CROWDED MARKETPLACE WERE MANY AND VARIED...

HA-HA-HA! DO YOU THINK US FOOLS TO FALL FOR A SHODDY *TRICK?*

HA HA HA!

DO ANY OF YOU *DARE* TO CHALLENGE ATLAS?

I, KARGIN, AM THE STRONGEST HERE!

IT IS THE *TRUTH!* ALL HYSSA KNOWS OF KARGIN!

YOU'LL CRUSH THIS ATLAS! CHALLENGE HIM, KARGIN.

THIS I SHALL *DO!*

COME, THEN. ATLAS *AWAITS* YOU!

KARGIN MOUNTS THE WOOD PLATFORM...

NO TRICK WILL SAVE YOU FROM KARGIN.

SUDDENLY!

WH....!!

4

HE *VANQUISHED* KARGIN!

WITH *ONE* BLOW!

ARE THERE NO *REWARDS* FOR SO MIGHTY A DEED? WOULD YOU WITHHOLD YOUR BOUNTY FROM ATLAS?

'TWAS TRULY *WORTH* SEEING.

CLINK!

I WAS *NOT* AMUSED, OUTSIDER! KARGIN WAS THE *VICTIM* OF SOME FOUL TREACHERY!

YES! T'WAS *FOUL PLAY!*

NAY, FOOLS!

TREACHEROUS DOGS!

BEGONE FROM THIS CITY!!

AT THAT MOMENT...

STEP ASIDE, RABBLE! YOU *BAR* OUR PATH!

WHO DARES TO *DELAY* A NOBLE OF THE KING?!

CLEAR THE WAY!!

6

THE SOLDIERS STRIKE!!!

WUMP!

WUMP!

WHA....!

KRAK!

KRAK!

YOU'LL ANSWER TO *ME* FOR THIS, STRANGER!

SO THE KING'S NOBLE WANTS AN *ANSWER*, EH?

HERE IT IS...*SIRE!*

WHAM!

7

DOG! YOU'LL PAY FOR THIS! WHO ARE YOU?

I AM ATLAS!

...AND I CARE LITTLE FOR POMPOUS WORMS WHO TRAVEL ON THE BACKS OF SLAVES!!

RELEASE ME!!

MIGHTY ATLAS IS DEAF TO THE THREATS OF HIS CAPTIVE...

THIS MEANS DEATH FOR YOU BOTH!

DROP HIM, ATLAS!! LET US FLEE THIS WRETCHED LAND!!

THEN...

IN THE KING'S NAME! ...HALT...OR WE SHOOT!!

NO! NO! WAIT...!

SHOOT! HERE IS A "NOBLE" TARGET FOR YOUR ARROWS!

AT THAT MOMENT, A VOICE INTERRUPTS THE STAND-OFF.....IT'S A LOW, REPTILIAN HISS OF A SOUND THAT JOLTS ATLAS.

WHAT KIND OF KNAVE'S WORK IS THIS??

THAT VOICE...! I'D KNOW IT ANYWHERE...!

ATLAS TURNS TO THE SOURCE OF THE SOUND....HE KNOWS THAT YEARS OF ENDLESS SEARCHING FOR ITS OWNER ARE ABOUT TO END...

THE FACE!! ATLAS SEES THE FACE!! ....AND TIME SUDDENLY RACES MADLY BACK TO THE PAST!!

THERE WAS ATLAS, THE CHILD....HIDDEN BY HIS PARENTS IN A CAVE DURING A MOMENT OF GREAT DANGER!

BURN THE VILLAGE! BURN IT DOWN!!!

NO!... NO!...

WE OBEY, MASTER!

THE SLAVERS SWOOPED DOWN LIKE A TERRIBLE SCOURGE!!

THIS WILL DRIVE OUR PREY FROM COVER.

9

THE CHILD ATLAS SAW HIS MOTHER CAPTURED WITH THE *OTHER* VILLAGERS.

LET NONE ESCAPE!

HIS FATHER RESISTED AGAINST OVERWHELMING ODDS...

STOP HIM!

HE'S LIKE A *TIGER*!

THEN, BEFORE HIS VERY EYES, ATLAS SAW HIS FATHER *STRUCK* DOWN.

WHAM!!

THE *GRIEF-STRICKEN* CHILD THEN RAN TO AID HIS FATHER.

Y-YOU HURT MY FATHER!!

SO THE TIGER HAS A *CUB*, EH?....*COME HERE!*

YOU......YOU...!

10

SUDDENLY, STARING DOWN AT A FRIGHTENED CHILD, WAS *THE FACE* THAT WOULD *CHANGE* ITS DESTINY....IT WAS THE FACE OF A HUMAN LIZARD....A CRUEL REPLICA OF THE CREST UPON ITS HELMET....THE CHILD, ATLAS, WOULD *NEVER* FORGET IT....THAT FACE WOULD MAKE HIM AN ETERNAL

AVENGER!

CHAPTER THREE

LET ME GO!

YOU'LL MAKE A *FIT* SLAVE ONE DAY, CUB!!

Y-YOU'RE **BAD**! I-I **HURT** YOU!! HA-HA-HA HA-HA-HA!!

THEN, TO THE SLAVER'S AMAZEMENT....

POW!

THE CHILD FELLED HIM WITH A **STRENGTH** BEYOND HIS YEARS...

SWIFT AS HE WAS STRONG, LITTLE ATLAS RACED TO A MARSH FOR SAFETY.

GET HIM! GET HIM!

THE MARSH WILL **HIDE** ME...

DO YOU **SEE** HIM?

WE'VE **LOST** HIM!!

SUDDENLY, FROM WITHIN THE MARSH...!

MAKE **NO** SOUND, BOY!

12

118

FREE ONCE AGAIN, THE CHILD RUSHED TO THE SCENE OF TRAGEDY... SEEKING HIS FATHER...

FATHER....! FATHER....!

...AND THEN HE FINDS HIS FATHER... *AMONG THE DEAD*...

IT'S TOO LATE, BRAT! THOSE SLAVERS SPARED *NO ONE*...

WHAT DOES THE BOY SEEK *NOW*? THE SLAVERS LEAVE NOTHING....NOTHING....

M-MY HOUSE.

HE IS A *STRANGE* CHILD. HIS STRENGTH IS THAT OF A *FULL-GROWN* MAN!!

CAN IT BE...?

...BUT *HOLD*...!

THE BOY RETURNS, BEARING A *GLOWING* OBJECT... A...A... *CRYSTAL*!!!

THE CRYSTAL POSSESSES A *THOUSAND* FACETS OF STABBING, MYSTIC LIGHT.

FORGIVE THIS *POOR* TRAVELER, BOY....LITTLE DID I REALIZE WHO YOUR *PEOPLE* WERE.

GO AWAY!

14

YOUR PEOPLE CAME FROM THE *CRYSTAL MOUNTAIN*...I KNOW THIS NOW FOR *TRUTH!*

...AND IT IS SAID THAT THE *LEADER* OF YOUR PEOPLE BEARS A PIECE OF THAT MOUNTAIN...AND MUST PASS IT ON...WHEN HE *DIES.*

I AM LEADER ...*NOW!!*

...*RIGHTLY* SO, BOY.

I AM *CHAGRA,* YOUR HUMBLE WITNESS AND LOYAL SUBJECT.... WHERE YOU LEAD,... I SHALL FOLLOW.

THE CHOICE IS *YOURS.*

CHAGRA FOLLOWED THE BOY, EVEN AS THE YEARS PASSED ...EVEN AS ATLAS GREW *LARGER* ...*STRONGER.*

EVEN INTO MANHOOD ...WHERE VENGEANCE HARDENED AND *LIVED.*

THE TWO SHARED TIMES OF GREAT HARDSHIP AND DANGER...

LOOK OUT! ...A GREAT BEAST!!

RRAAWR!

15

121

It was the **BEGINNING** of a great destiny....it was the shaping of a giant figure whose shadow would fall across **ALL** of mankind.....and, one day, as the world grew older, his name would **STILL** live whenever men spoke of **AWESOME** deeds....yet, the living atlas sought only the road which led to a

HUMAN LIZARD!

CHAPTER
FOUR

UGH!

KKRUMP!

16

THE MUSCLE AND SINEW OF ATLAS WERE A **MATCH** FOR ANYTHING THAT ROAMED.... HE HURLED BACK THE BEAST!

KILL IT, ATLAS! ...KILL IT!

NO, CHAGRA.

IT IS A YOUNG BEAST.... AND **FAR** FROM ITS KIN.

BUT THERE WERE WITNESSES TO THIS FEAT!

SUCH MIGHT I HAVE **NEVER** SEEN.

WE MUST **TELL** OF THIS TO OTHERS.

SURELY, HE IS A MAN OF **DESTINY**.

HE HOLDS THE BRIDGE UPON HIS BACK.

IT IS ATLAS! HE **SAVED** OUR LIVES!

HEROIC DEEDS WERE TO BE THE MARK OF ATLAS.

IN A LAND OF **DEVIL-WORSHIP**, IT WAS ATLAS WHO DESTROYED THE IDOL "ISHTAK"!

THERE SHALL BE NO MORE VICTIMS FOR YOU, EVIL ONE!

17

IN THE FIGHTING ARENAS BUILT BY BARBARIC PRINCES, ATLAS GAINED *MORE* RENOWN BY DISPATCHING SQUADS OF TRAINED KILLERS.

HAIL, ATLAS! HAIL, ATLAS!

CRUNCH!

H-HE *CAN'T* BE STOPPED!

VICTORY FOLLOWED VICTORY...ATLAS WON TROPHIES AND GIFTS.

HAIL! HAIL!

THE GOLDEN "HELMET OF CHAMPIONS" IS YOURS, ATLAS!

ATLAS WON NO RICHES...BUT HE *SOON* HAD *GOOD* TRANSPORTATION AND SUPPLIES FOR CHAGRA AND HIMSELF.

IT'S A LONG ROAD, ATLAS, IT LIES EVER *AHEAD*.

AHEAD LIES WHAT I *SEEK*!

18

THEN, ONE NIGHT, CHAGRA CONFESSED...

I'VE WAITED UNTIL YOU WERE READY TO BARGAIN, ATLAS....I CAN LEAD *YOU* TO *YOUR* GOAL ....IF YOU.... LEAD *ME* TO THE *CRYSTAL MOUNTAIN.*

I SEE.... THEN *FIRST* TO THE LIZARD KINGDOM!

THE BARGAIN WAS STRUCK. DAYS LATER, THE PAIR *ENTERED* THE FORBIDDEN REGION OF FIRE....

NOTHING CAN LIVE HERE!!

THIS LAND IS RAVAGED BY *HEAT* AND *FLAME.*

NOT IN THIS SPOT. IT IS AN *ILLUSION* MADE TO DECEIVE MEN'S SENSES.

THEN THE TALES OF FIRE WIZARDS ARE *TRUE.*

WITHOUT FEAR OR HESITATION, CHAGRA RODE THROUGH THE FLAMES....ATLAS FOLLOWED.

ARE *YOU* SUCH A WIZARD, CHAGRA?

NO, BUT I LIVED IN THIS ACCURSED KINGDOM.

THEN THERE FELL THE *DISMAL* GLOOM OF A GIANT CAVERN....ITS CLAMMY WALLS WERE OLD....OLD AS TIME ITSELF.

NOW YOU RISK ALL TO *DEFY* ITS SECRET ...AND *RETURN* HERE.

HONOR OUR BARGAIN. *THAT'S* ALL I ASK.

19

THERE WERE **STRANGE** ECHOES IN THIS HOARY DOMAIN....SOUNDS OF THINGS **LONG** THOUGHT TO HAVE VANISHED....

HHRRRSSS!!

WHAT WAS THAT?

RIDE ON, ATLAS.

THE REMEMBERED SOUND OF THE LIZARD JOLTS THE THOUGHTS OF ATLAS **FORWARD** TO HIS GOAL'S END....

HOLD, KNAVE!

I'VE FOUND IT! THE FACE THAT'S HAUNTED ME...THE VOICE...

I AM HYSSA....WHAT MANNER OF FOOL DARES TO MISTREAT ONE WHOM I FAVOR!!?

HYSSA LOOKS DEEP INTO THE EYES OF ATLAS...AND GROWS **UNEASY**....

HAVE WE NOT MET BEFORE?

SPEAK! WHO ARE YOU!!?

YOUR CONQUEROR!

20

THUS, A GREAT SAGA BEGINS!!